Welcome back friends!

In *this book*, we will discuss current trends in the online sales industry and look at recent updates to the Amazon marketplace to see how they affect store owners.

We will also expand upon several aspects of selling on Mercari that shop owners have asked for more discussion on via Facebook groups and on our blog.

There are a number of other books that offer internet selling tips on Kindle. Many of these "guides" are ghost-written by "authors" that have never sold an item online. Many of the books cover only one aspect of selling online.

Information products similar to *this book* are being offered online for hundreds of dollars. I do not believe in gouging fellow sellers like that. I provide this information at an extremely affordable cost. In return, all I ask is three things:

1. Leave a positive review on the Amazon book page and on Goodreads.com. The income earned from these books is used for my two boys' college funds.
2. Share this book through your social media outlets and word-of-mouth.
3. Put this information to good use and don't wait to start making money! People who wait for next week usually never end up getting started at all.

In this book, I will explain exactly how I have set up my Mercari account for success. Remember, the great thing about the Almost Free Money books is that as soon as you sell that *first additional item,* you have already made profit on your book order! Where else can you say that about any investment?

Benefits gained from reading this book:

1. Take your used item selling to the next level and start down the road toward making a full-time income doing what you love.

2. Read about the newest trends on Mercari.com and how they will increase your income from selling used items online.

I am excited to share my story with you and get you out there looking for inventory, so you can start making some money. But first, we need to lay out the game plan for this book and discuss reader expectations for the topics that will be covered here.

What you will get from this book:

1. In this book, we are going to start from scratch and build a large Mercari inventory that earns you a significant e-check that goes into your bank account whenever you choose.

2. We will go through the basics of selling on Mercari. Even if you have never been on Mercari's website or app, you will be able to start selling on Mercari. You will know how to list inventory items and process orders and collect your money from Mercari.

3. I will teach you everything that you need to know to research which types of inventory items to sell. You can figure out for yourself which road is right for you. You should sell in categories that you are familiar with and/or enjoy working in.

4. I will tell you exactly what I have sold on Mercari and why those items worked for me.

5. We will discuss managing your inventory and effective pricing of inventory items, so that your inventory sells quickly, and you have more money to increase the size of your inventory.

6. As we proceed through this book, I will provide you with some resources that will help you to build your background knowledge, learn Mercari selling techniques, and find new categories of inventory items in which to sell.

What you will NOT get from this book:

1. A get-rich-quick plan. Although I started selling items within several days of finding my first inventory item, it does take considerable time and effort to build an Mercari inventory that provides a regular and significant semi-passive income. You will also have to re-build your inventory as your items sell. This is a home business, and you will have to work at it to be successful. After reading this book, you will have the advantage of hearing

what worked for me, but you will still have to apply the knowledge that you learned and work as hard as I did to build a comparable inventory. Nothing is given to you in this world. If you are not willing to work, do not read any further.

2. This is not an Mercari selling primer. We will cover everything you need to know to build your inventory and maintain your business effectively. But, Mercari does an excellent job of providing sellers all the background information that they need to run their business on a day-to-day level. Their Seller Help pages are very easy to understand and navigate.

There. Now we have laid the guidelines for this book. Now let's get the basics out of the way, so we can get to the fun stuff – shopping for great items to put in your Amazon inventory!

Chapter Summary:

Benefits of reading this book:

1. Build a semi-passive income that generates consistent and profitable paychecks
2. Learn Mercari selling basics. Start listing items immediately.
3. How I buy low and sell high on Mercari
4. How to build your Mercari business and manage your inventory for maximum sales
5. Learn how to research new income sources
6. Links to vital how-to pages on the internet

What this book is not:

1. An Mercari selling instructional book
2. A get-rich-quick book

ABOUT THE AUTHOR

Eric Michael is married and is a proud father of two energetic sons. He enjoys family outings and many outdoor activities, including fishing, hunting and camping.

The information provided in this book and in the Almost Free Money series was compiled during fifteen years of selling goods on the internet from home and related internet research. His personal experiences have developed a unique skill set – the ability to find a diverse selection of free items (or priced under $1) that can be sold on the internet for at surprisingly good profit margins.

Eric Michael was recently featured in Woman's World magazine as an 'Ultimate Expert' regarding selling used items on the internet for profit.

Almost Free Money series books have been #1 Kindle bestsellers in 12 different categories and sold tens of thousands of copies. Currently, there are three AFM books in the Top 10 list in the Auctions and Small Businesses category on Amazon.

Mr. Michael has gone on to develop two popular websites - EricMichaelBooks.com and Garage Sale Academy. He also hosts Facebook fan pages for Almost Free Money and Garage Sale Academy.

'Almost Free Money' books for Internet Resellers:

1) Almost Free Money, Volume 1 FREE! (#1 Kindle bestseller, Top 10 for 3 years running). Learn how to find over 500 different types of items for free where you live and sell for profit online and at scrap metal locations for big bucks.
2) Thrift Wars (#1 Kindle Bestseller): Learn how professional sellers locate the best items to resell from thrift stores for very high profit margins. Learn how to sell on Amazon, Etsy and eBay for maximum profit margins.
3) Etsy Empire (#1 Kindle and Softcover bestseller, top 10 for 24 months straight): How to build a powerful Etsy shop and sell handmade and collectible items on Etsy.com. Master Etsy SEO, social media for Etsy and Etsy marketing with a proven step-by-step formula.
4) Amazon Seller Academy (#1 Kindle Bestseller) How to set up and build a large Amazon and Amazon FBA business selling used goods and/or arbitrage goods. Valuable tips on the best categories of items to sell and how to dramatically increase sales prices.
5) Etsy Empire Strikes Back (#1 Kindle Bestseller): Advanced techniques for marketing with social media, like Facebook, Instagram and Pinterest, plus the latest Etsy shop rules and updates

6) Almost Free Gold: (#1 Kindle bestseller, top 10 for 24 months straight): Learn how to find valuable gold and silver jewelry for cheap at garage sales and thrift stores. You can also learn how to harvest free gold and silver from junk sources in this fun and unique approach to earning income!
7) The Almost Free Money Triple Play Value Pack: Contains the three bestselling AFM books: Almost Free Money, Passive Income for Life and Garage Sale Superstar. A great bargain!

Table of Contents

ABOUT THE AUTHOR

WHY MERCARI?

MERCARI SELLING BASICS

OK… NOW, HOW DO I FIGURE OUT WHAT TO SELL?

HOW TO BUILD AN IMPRESSIVE INVENTORY

THE MERCARI LISTING PAGE: WHAT YOU MUST KNOW

MERCARI SHIPPING

MERCARI PHOTOGRAPHY

CATEGORIES OF USED ITEMS TO SELL

INCREASE PROFITS AND SELL ITEMS FASTER BY MAKING BETTER ITEM DESCRIPTIONS ON MERCARI

MERCARI PRICING AND INVENTORY MANAGEMENT PRACTICES THAT YIELD MORE MERCARI SALES

CUSTOMER RELATIONS PRACTICES AND MAINTAINING A HIGH CUSTOMER FEEDBACK PERCENTAGE

HOW TO INCREASE SALES PRICE AND THE NUMBER OF SOLD ITEMS – MERCARI SELLING TIPS

WHAT NOT TO DO ON MERCARI: TERMS OF SERVICE AND VIOLATIONS

DIVERSIFYING YOUR MERCARI BUSINESS: SELLING PRODUCTS ON AMAZON, CRAIGSLIST, EBAY AND ETSY

ADDITIONAL LINKS FOR FURTHER RESEARCH

THANK YOU, READERS!

Thrift Wars: *A Battle-Tested Internet Business Plan: Find Hidden Thrift Stores Treasure and Sell on Amazon, eBay and Etsy for Huge Profits with Online Arbitrage* is now updated on Amazon Kindle.

WHY MERCARI?

Before we start discussing why you should sell on Mercari and its benefits, we should first define the platform a bit for those sellers that are unfamiliar with it.

Mercari is quite different than the traditional internet powerhouse resale sites like Amazon, Etsy and eBay. Mercari is almost entirely app-based. Sellers list items from smart phones and devices.

The platform advertises itself as selling marketplace app for individual people, rather than an outlet for resellers and retail arbitrage sellers. However, the relatively young site (launched in 2013) is very popular with the millennial generation and current high schoolers, so certain categories of trending items often sell very quickly and at higher prices than on eBay (and sometimes even Amazon FBA – more on types of items to sell on Mercari in a later chapter).

If you are the type of seller that prefers using technology and expediting the listing process, then Mercari should be just your ticket! Of all of sites that I have listed on, Mercari is the easiest and quickest site to list new listings on. Just snap a photo of the item, pick categories from easy drop-down lists (and often Mercari will recognize popular items and prepopulate some of the entries) and type a quick description and bang, you're live!

The selling fees on Mercari are also a straight 10% charge on the ending sales price of the item. There are no extra PayPal fees. Plus, there are no listing fees. There are unlimited numbers of free listings per month and no PayPal issues – Bonus!

Mercari is probably the fastest-growing internet sales site in the United States and it is already the #1 internet sales site in Japan, where app designer and owner Shintaro Yamada built the company into a 10 billion JPY a year business. The Mercari app, which has been downloaded to cellular devices over 100 million times, has been voted Best App of the Year three times by Google Play.

I found Mercari by accident… kind of. I was researching new sources of used items to look for by typing in Google searches. Time after time, I was seeing collectibles and trending items from Mercari sellers in the top two or three results on Google Shopping and I thought to myself, how do I not know about this? After a little bit of background checking, I was selling items on Mercari that same week.

To make a long story short, Mercari is an impressive shopping app and one that serious sellers should take advantage of, especially if it continues to grab internet marketplace influence with young people. This holiday season is the perfect time to add a new and budding revenue source to your already growing internet business!

Chapter Summary:

Why Mercari:

1. New and growing internet marketplace
2. Easy and free to list items
3. Selling fees flat 10% - cheaper than eBay (at time of this book's publication)

MERCARI SELLING BASICS

Here is the complete process of selling an item on Mercari:

1) Log into your Mercari account. If you do not have a Mercari account, all you have to do is download the app to your cellular device from Google Play store or iTunes App store. Then, enter your personal information and confirm your account with the provided confirm code and you are ready to sell. The new account verification process only takes a couple of minutes.

2) On your cellular device open the Mercari app. Click the orange Sell button.

3) One of the best features of the Mercari app is the photo upload function. It is fast and easy compared to other platforms' listing procedures. Just click on the Add Photo squares to upload directly from your phone's camera, if you want to list items that you have at the time. Or, you can upload photos from your device's file manager if you have saved photos that you would prefer to use. This makes it ideal to list items on Mercari that you have already listed on other sites.

4) Provide the title, condition and a short description of your item, list your price, shipping selection and make it available for sale. Congratulations! Your item is now listed on Mercari and available for purchase on the site in minutes. It took you about 30 seconds to list it, right? Welcome to the power of Mercari.

5) When your item sells on Mercari, you are sent a notification on your device (unless you choose to turn off notifications) and an email to your registered email address notifying you of the sale.

6)   Prepare your item for shipment and then open the sold item email from Mercari. If you chose the prepaid Mercari shipping label, all you have to do is download the image and print it. Stick it on the package and drop it off at the post office or have your mail carrier pick it up.

7) When the customer receives your item, the seller must rate the buyer and then your proceeds from the sale are released to your account, minus the 10% Mercari selling fee. Awesome! You just sold your first item on Mercari and it took about five minutes of your time.

We will get into the nuts and bolts of how to correctly list and ship items, how to increase sales profits with great photos and descriptions and customer relations procedures in subsequent chapters of *Mercari Magic*. But for now, you learned how to sell on Mercari and are prepared to make some money! CHAAA-CHING!

Chapter Summary:

How to start selling on Mercari:

1. Downloading Mercari app and setting up account
2. Step by step process for listing an item for sale on Mercari.com

OK... NOW, HOW DO I FIGURE OUT WHAT TO SELL?

The most important thing that an internet seller can do to increase earnings and profit margins earned on inventory items sold is to learn how to research. The learning process should be a continuous effort. Learning about new sources of inventory and methods for improving business procedures should not wane after you become an experienced seller.

The internet sales landscape is always evolving. Technology makes used items obsolete or undesirable. Consumer appetites change and the demand for pop culture media items can decline rapidly. Sellers have to be able to adjust to these changes accordingly. This is where research is vital. As a seller, you have to know what consumers are buying and how much they are willing to pay for items.

There are a variety of places that can help you to determine what types of items are hot, and what other sellers are doing well with. Social media is probably the easiest way to research current trends. There is a lot of information on Facebook and Twitter. There are groups dedicated to talking about selling on Mercari, eBay, Amazon and Etsy.

There are several very nice features on the Mercari app that helps see what is hot. Right on the Home page of the app, sellers are provided with two modules with photos of the items along with their prices. At the top of the app is 'Sold in the last 10 minutes' and a little bit below that is 'Just In'. These are great places to spend some time and see what a lot of sellers are selling and what range of process to list your items in for quick sales or best profits.

As I write this book, Funko Pop toys, Rae Dunn décor items and the latest generation of video game consoles and accessories are smoking hot on Mercari. The items that are the most popular on Mercari can sell in minutes and at higher prices than on other sites. But, it is also important to note that everyday used items that you have around your house can sell very well on Mercari, too. I have done well selling newer books (especially if you have several related books that you can sell as a book lot), kids name brand toys (think Legos, Marvel, popular board games, electronic games, etc.), used shoes in very good condition, seasonal clothes and holiday décor items.

You could also conduct a simple search on Google or Bing search engines for 'sell used items', or a similar search query and you will have dozens of free sources of information. There are also some excellent Kindle books devoted to the topic.

Our website EricMichaelBooks.com also has many FREE pages that can assist sellers with finding inventory and also learning how to improve listings and develop good business practices. Among the topics with devoted webpages: How to sell on Mercari, Etsy and Amazon, Amazon packaging and shipping, how to sell used books, CDs, DVDs, video games, collectibles and used clothes, how to sell textbooks, how to find the best items at garage sales, thrift stores and flea markets. There are also many links provided that direct readers to the best free niche sites related to selling used items.

Chapter Summary:

- The value and importance of research
- Demand for Mercari items changes frequently

Where to start researching types of used items to sell

1. Mercari Items Sold and Just Listed sections
2. Internet searches and search engine queries
3. Social Media
4. www.EricMichaelBooks.com

HOW TO BUILD AN IMPRESSIVE INVENTORY

I started selling used items for profit about 18 years ago. At that time, there was significantly less competition. It was easy to find treasure at garage sales and sell the items on eBay for excellent profit margins.

For the first five years of my business, I sold primarily used collectibles and media items on eBay, and I did well. Over time, several things happened. #1, I got tired of spending all of my time making eBay auctions, and #2, profit margins on eBay shrank as more and more internet sellers discovered how easy it was to sell used items and collectibles on eBay.

It became harder and harder to find quality collectibles at second-hand locations and eBay was getting tougher to sell effectively on. Besides that, eBay continually increased their selling fees and changed their customer feedback structure so that it made it very hard to keep your seller feedback rating high unless you were a high volume seller.

Many collectible item auctions were also ending without a bid. I got tired of paying eBay listing fees and getting little in return, in many cases. So, I started looking for other ways to diversify my used item sales. Almost immediately, I discovered selling used items on Amazon.

When I first started selling on Amazon, very few sellers sold used items there. As a matter of fact, very few internet sellers even knew that it was possible to sell used items on Amazon. Heck yeah, I thought. Amazon is a huge marketplace, with less competition than on eBay, and you don't even have to pay listing fees (as on eBay). Let's do this!

My only concern at the time was trying to decide if my efforts would be worthwhile, because I did not know if there would be enough demand on Amazon for the used items that I was finding at garage sales, thrift stores, and other second-hand locations.

I found out quickly that selling on Amazon was significantly more efficient and profitable than eBay for the types of items that I wanted to sell. I still make at least 60% of my profits on Amazon, but my Etsy shop and Mercari store are increasing in sales and profits faster than my older and more established Amazon business.

Mercari is an important part of my internet selling business, as it allows me to sell a whole new range of items. Remember, I can't stand eBay, so Mercari allows me to sell things that I could not sell on Amazon (most used clothes are prohibited) and Etsy (must be 15+ years old), like newer used clothes and home décor items. It also allows me to move certain types of items very quickly. My sons recently had their Xbox One system die on them, so I sold the console for parts on Mercari for $60, which was more than I thought than I would earn for the broken system. I also listed the controllers, power cord and 10 games on both Mercari and Amazon at the same time and all but one game sold on Mercari first for several dollars a piece more than what they were listed for on Amazon.

I have also used Mercari to sell quite a few items that were in my Amazon and Etsy inventories for years. Stuff that is a little bit funky or eclectic can sell very well on Mercari, where many younger customers shop. As we all know, younger buyers tend to make more impulse buys online, when compared to older shoppers who grew up shopping in brick and mortar stores, where it was easier to sticker shop.

Chapter Summary:

How I started building my $50,000 internet selling business

- Prior experience selling on other sites
- Adding new platforms
- Why Mercari is important for sales diversification

THE MERCARI LISTING PAGE: WHAT YOU MUST KNOW

We are going to get to the fun part of this book soon – the portion of the book where we talk about how to increase profits and build a powerhouse Mercari presence. But first, there are some things that you must know to run your Mercari business. DO NOT skip this part!

The easiest way to cover the important topics that we have to discuss is to go section by section from the Mercari item listing page. It will be much easier for you to understand what I am talking about if you open the Mercari app and list an item. It can be anything… a used CD, some jeans that don't fit right… whatever.

OK, great. You are back and ready to follow along, so let's roll.

Let's start at the top of the item listing page.

Photos: You can upload up to eight photos in jpg format. Having good item photos is vital, so that will be covered in detail in a separate chapter. But, make sure that you include a bare minimum of two photos – one close enough, so customers can see the condition of the item and one photo from further away that provides perspective and allows the customer to see the entire item in one photo.

It's very important to select the main item photo (the first one uploaded, or the furthest to the left on the photo bar) that will earn the most views from customers. Make sure that the best part of the item is visible in the main photo, including the brand name on popular items like Nike shoes, Under Armor shirts, etc.

Ensure that your photos are in focus, have proper lighting and highlight the part of the item that appeals most to the customer. Mercari Terms of Service (TOS) prevents any photos that could be deemed offensive or sexually explicit, so don't risk getting suspended by using photos that are too suggestive – Mercari is conservative, when it comes right down to it.

Title: You can have up to 40 characters in the item's title, including the spaces. Mercari is more of a visual shopping experience than Etsy or eBay. The titles of the items are not seen from the Buying browsing page – only the main item photo and the price are displayed.

However, the title is still the most important part of your item, when it comes to search engine optimization (SEO) for both the Mercari Buying marketplace and Google. The title is also a shopping verification for your buyer – if the title does not specify what the item is, many shoppers will not read the description and you will lose the sale.

Important tips for your item titles:

- Include the entire title of the item, when possible. Think about what shoppers will be typing into a search bar to find your item. In other words, don't use only popular abbreviations of popular video games, like using COD for Call of Duty games. If you can fit the popular abbreviation along with the longer title, I would include it, though. You want to try to include the main search terms that people type into a search bar in your title. My title for a COD Xbox One game would be 'Call of Duty Modern Warfare Xbox One COD' (40 characters). Other sellers will often shorten the most important SEO words to enable them to include that the game has the case or is in VG condition, etc. This is a mistake that will end up costing you thousands of page views.
- Put the most important SEO aspects first. If you are trying to sell a red Nike hoodie sweatshirt size Men's XL. Don't use this title: Men's XL Red Sweatshirt Nike. Use this: Nike Hoodie Sweatshirt Men's XL. People search for 'Nike Hoodie' and 'Hoodie Sweatshirt', so you want those exact words in your title.
- Spell words and brand names correctly. This should be common sense, but I see spelling errors in titles all the time. Not only does spelling errors negatively affect SEO, it also reduces consumer confidence in you as a seller. Do want to buy a used item from somebody that doesn't care enough about the item to spell it right? I don't.
- If you have extra characters left, add words that people search for instead of descriptive words. Seasonal gifts and holiday words can be used around the holidays like Christmas, Mother's Day and Father's Day.

Photos: Provide up to 8 photos of your item. Upload .jpg files from your phone or laptop photo files or take photos as you list your item and upload directly to Mercari as you go. More on photos in a later chapter.

Category: Choose the category that best fits your item from the drop-down lists or even easier, use the search bar within the category feature and Mercari will show you the options for best category based on SEO for the app. Often, the category is selected for you based on keywords in your title or recognition of items in your photos. You can always change it to your own selection, if you like.

Brand: Brand is also often auto-filled, based on your title and/or photos. Again, you can use the search function, which takes much less time than scrolling the list and finding the correct brand. Most of the choices are for high profile and current clothing brands, so if you are selling collectibles, books, etc., you will usually end selecting 'No Brand'.

Condition: Choose from the five offered condition boxes – New, Like New, Good, Far, Poor. Each box has a brief qualifying description that help you to determine the correct condition. BE CONSERVATIVE when choosing the condition of your items. Nothing will get you a negative rating or suspension faster than trying to game the system and listing items that are used as New or even Like New. You cannot sell items that you find at a second-hand location as either New or Like New, unless the item is factory sealed. Don't be tempted to re-package or re-seal an open package and sell as New or Like New. It's against Mercari's terms of service and could even be illegal (fraud).

Note that the Like New condition on Mercari's selling page is not the same as Amazon's or eBay's conditions. To be Like New on Mercari, the item must be unused, with no signs of wear at all. Basically, the item must be brand new, with only the tags removed. If you have an item that is missing the original packaging, like the original box or outer wrapping, the item should be listed as 'Good', not 'Like New'.

Again, it is a good practice to select the condition that is one level lower than what you think that the item qualifies for, to allow for picky buyers. If you are not sure, move down a level, not up. If your item is missing any pieces, or is not 100% functional, it should not be listed as 'Good'. It's very important to keep your seller rating at (or very close to) 100% five-star customer ratings, so judge your item categories accordingly.

Description: The item description is the second most important section on the listing page, after the photos, yet many sellers provide buyers only one line of information to make their buying description. Don't be lazy! You also should not be in a hurry to pump out a bunch of listings in the shortest amount of time. Taking an extra minute to give the potential customer the reassurance that your item is what they are looking for will yield a much higher percentage of sell-through listings and they will sell faster, with fewer price drops.

We will get into more detail in the Tips chapter, but at a bare minimum your description should have two paragraphs. The first paragraph is a confirmation of what the item is, so the customer knows exactly what they are getting. Often, you cannot fit the entire item definition in the title because of the 40-character restriction. So, in the first paragraph of the description, you should tell the customer exactly what the item is

– Brand, full name of the item, size for clothing, platform for video games, the year of manufacture for collectibles, items included in group listing, etc. You should provide specific information on what is included with your listing – do electronics have all the cords? Does the book have a dust jacket? Does the collectible item have the original box? DON'T rely on your photos to let customers know what is included in your listing. Spelling out exactly what the item is does three things: First, it's a CYA (cover your a**) against chargebacks and complaints. Customers can't file legitimate claims of misrepresentation, if you told them right in the description that the item was a cassette and not a CD, or that a certain accessory was not included.

Second, buying confidence is very important to sell-through. A confirmation in text form of the visual representation of the item's photos will inspire more buy clicks, especially if you craft your descriptions in the manner that we will discuss later.

Third, the text of the item description is used for Mercari SEO, so it is another way to get your item displayed to the right buyers, which is another reason to use the whole item title (with brand names) and any popular abbreviations for the item in the description.

The second paragraph should be used for the item's condition description. It is vital to be accurate here and give your buyer a complete run-down of the items' condition, even if the item is New and sealed, I still provide a quick line stating that to buyers and confirm that the box is not damaged and there are not stickers all over the box. Again, DO NOT rely on Mercari's small description box to describe your item's description. I see many lazy sellers who say simply 'condition per Mercari standards'. What does that mean?!

It only takes 30 seconds to provide exact condition descriptions, so that your buyer knows exactly what they are getting. Put yourself in your buyers' shoes. What would you want to know about the item's condition? Does the electronic item work? Does it have all the cords? Are toys complete, with accessories? What kind of wear does the used item have? Is anything missing or not original parts? Look your item over carefully and then double check before you submit your listing. Are there any hairline cracks in collectible glass items? Are there any small pieces missing from toys? Do all the buttons and functions of the item work as intended?

I try to avoid using descriptors that are value terms or are subjective adjectives, to prevent discrepancies in values. In other words, a would not say "jacket is a little dirty". I would say "visual soiling along waist line, as seen in photo 2". That way, customers cannot argue with your value assessment.

The last two lines of the condition description is very important. ALWAYS tell the buyer if your used item came from a 'Smoke-Free' home. There are many buyers who want to know that information – some people just cannot handle any smoking smell and there are others who are allergic to it. Similarly, you should describe the pet situation in your home, if you are selling items that belonged to your family. Many people are allergic to certain animals and there are others who just do not like any hint of pet smells. This is especially important for clothing and fabrics, but it applies to everything. I always include the line 'From a smoke-free, one dog upscale home' in my condition description, if I am selling used items from my family's home. If I am selling items from a second-hand location (thrift store, yard sale), I wash any fabrics and then describe any smells, especially if there is any hint of smoking odors.

The last line should be an attempt to "grab the buy-click". Get your buyer excited about your item. "These boots are super warm and comfortable for long winter play days!" or "All the neighbor kids came over to play this game" or "These items are jumping off our shelves – HOT! (for items where you sell multiple versions, etc.)

Hashtags: At the bottom of the description box is a line where you can add up to three hashtags. Use all three hashtags, as they are opportunities for SEO, via popular tags. I always use one hashtag for Mercari + the type of item, as in #MercariXboxone, or #Mercaribooks. Hashtags are another opportunity to let buyers find your item, so use terms that are not in your title. For a Call of Duty Xbox One game, I might use: #COD #Xboxonegame #Mercarixboxone for my three hashtags. Remember, there are no spaces in hashtag text, just like on Twitter and Instagram. Use the hashtag (#) and then the text, with no spaces at all. These hashtags are also supposed to be used for SEO outside of Mercari, via Twitter and Instagram searches and through Google, but I have not been able to confirm how effective Mercari's reach outside the platform is.

Shipping: This will also be covered in its own chapter, but here you enter the zip code that you are shipping from and whether you or the buyer are paying for shipping. If the buyer is paying for shipping, you have two options. Either the seller pays for shipping (the shipping cost is included in the item's price), or the buyer pays for shipping (the shipping cost is added in after the sale, on top of the item price).

Mercari calculates shipping by weight and seller location and provides sellers two methods for shipping. First (and easiest), Mercari provides sellers a Mercari shipping label at a specified cost for both USPS and FedEx shipping (seller's choice as to shipping company). When your item sells, the buyer pays for the item. Then, Mercari sends you an email with an attached shipping label, which you print out and attach to your package before shipment.

After you have completed one sale, Mercari also offers sellers the ability to use their own shipping method, instead of using the standard Mercari shipping label. I use this option if it is significantly cheaper to ship the item another way besides the FedEx, First Class or Priority Mail methods offered by Mercari. For instance, when I ship groups of books or vinyl records, I ship them USPS Bound-Printed Matter or Media Mail via PayPal shipping, because it saves $5-10 in shipping fees and allows the items to be listed at a price that makes the item much more likely to sell. More on this in the Mercari Shipping chapter.

Set Price: This is where you offer the price for your item. This is the base price, from which Mercari will subtract a 10% selling fee from each sale. Also, if you chose 'You' for shipping options, you will also have to pay for shipping costs from that price when your item sells. Mercari has a mandatory minimum of $5 per item. You cannot list an item for under that amount and you cannot exceed $2000. We will talk about pricing strategies in a subsequent chapter, as well.

Once you have filled in all the listing boxes, you can click 'LIST'. Time to make some money, Baby!

Chapter Summary:

Important notes about the Mercari listing page:

- The most important thing is not initial sales. Start building your inventory and worry about the number of sales later.
- Start by getting used items for free or buying at very low prices
- Sell free items that you already have in your home
- Look for 'high-profit' items
- Buy cheap items at garage sales and thrift stores.
- Look for large lots of low priced items to break up into single Amazon inventory items
- Flipping eBay listings to Amazon – Lots and Single items

MERCARI SHIPPING

Shipping sold Mercari items is simple, but there are some things that you must know before you list items. If you are not paying attention when you fill out the shipping section on the item listing form, you can lose profits from your sale or worse, you could not get paid for your completed sale!

First, let's talk about the shipping basics. When you first sign up to sell on Mercari, you only have two shipping options. The first option is to have the customer pay for shipping on top of the item cost, using the Mercari prepaid shipping label. When you list your item, you must input your item's weight – 0-1 LB, 1-3 LBs, 3-10 LBs, etc. Then, you choose whether to use USPS or FedEx shipping (the cost is displayed below each choice).

The second option is to offer free shipping and have the seller pay for the shipping cost by subtracting the shipping cost from the sale price of the item. If you offer free shipping with this method, you still enter the same information that you enter when you use the prepaid label.

When your item is purchased, Mercari sends the seller an email notifying you of the sale. Attached to the email is an attachment that contains a shipping label. All you have to do is print the label and attach it to the package that is being shipped to your customer. If you chose to have the customer pay for the shipping fees, the shipping cost is paid for when the customer makes payment for the item. If you chose free shipping, the shipping cost is subtracted from the profit earned from the sale when the item is received by your customer.

After you have completed one sale on Mercari, sellers are also allowed to use a third shipping method – Ship on your own. If you choose this option, you must pay for shipping outside of Mercari. This is similar to offering free shipping with the prepaid label shipping. You include the shipping cost of the item into the price of the item. When the item sells, you pay for shipping via a shipping provider (USPS, FedEx, UPS) and attach that label to your package before shipping it.

PAY ATTENTION HERE: If you use the 'Ship your own' option, YOU MUST USE PACKAGE TRACKING / DELIVERY CONFIRMATION. When you buy your shipping label, you will be provided a tracking number on the label. You must enter that package tracking number when you notify Mercari that you shipped the item out to your customer. Mercari Terms of Service require that all packages sent to buyers MUST have a tracking number, so that Mercari can ensure delivery of the item. This is not an option that sellers can choose whether to use package tracking or not (there is a small cost to add tracking for some classes of shipping labels). If you do not provide Mercari with the tracking number for the package that you ship to your customer, you will not get paid at all for the sale transaction, if the customer does not notify Mercari that they received the package. This happens a lot, when customers rely on the Mercari system to automatically close out the sale.

In other words, you could sell a video game system for $200 on Mercari. If you chose to use your own shipping label and did not record the tracking number, you could end up paying $25 to ship the item to your buyer and NOT RECEIVE A PENNY for the item because it did not have tracking information provided. ALWAYS use tracking / delivery confirmation on your packages!

For most types of items sold on Mercari, I use the prepaid USPS shipping labels when I ship items. It is the easiest method and it usually does not increase the shipping costs vs other outside-Mercari shipping methods.

I do use the 'Ship on your own' option for several types of packages. Items that qualify for steeply discounted USPS shipping options such as Media Mail Bound Printed Matter and heavy items that can fit in Flat Rate Priority Mail envelopes can result in higher Mercari sales prices and seller profits by opting out of the prepaid Mercari labels. This is because the steeply discounted shipping allows you to reduce the cost of shipping by a significant amount, which results in customers feeling more comfortable purchasing the item at a higher sticker price.

There are several ways to buy your own shipping – remember, you included the cost of the shipping in your item's sticker price, right? First, you can take your package to the post office or FedEx store and buy a label there. I print my postage from the PayPal using the Create a Shipping Label function at https://www.paypal.com/shiplabel/create. This allows you to create a USPS shipping label (for any USPS mail class) using your PayPal balance, which is great if you also sell on eBay or Etsy and carry a balance on PayPal.

If you are just starting out in internet sales, you will have to invest in a digital postage scale. I recommend a scale that weighs items up to at least fifty pounds and gives you fractional ounces. This will run you about $20-50, depending on whether you buy the scale new or used. A couple of things that are handy options with digital scales are having a detachable digital display so that you can see the weight when you are weighing large bulky boxes and having a lithium battery scale, so your scale is mobile and does not have to be plugged in or charged.

Don't guess on the weight of your listed items! It can cost you a lot of profit over the course of your selling career. If you are using the prepaid labels, you will get to know how much frequently sold items weigh – single CDs are 4-5 ounces, Xbox games are about six ounces, etc. Just make sure you weigh items that are close to the cut-off values, such as items that weigh right around a pound. Don't be lazy and guess on an item's weight and have that item returned to you for having insufficient postage, which will result in poor seller ratings (due to late delivery) and more packages getting lost in the USPS system.

Also, you will also want to weigh your item inside the padding and box that you will be shipping it in after it sells. Sometimes, large boxes can add over a pound to the overall weight of your item when it is shipped. It is important to include that additional cost into your shipping calculations. Even small boxes and envelopes can occasionally push your package into the next higher shipping level (i.e. 1-3 LBs, instead of under 1 LB).

Printing Shipping Labels: Printing the Mercari shipping labels is very easy. Simply download the label from the sold item email and click print. Then, firmly tape the label onto your package and ship it out.

A little tip: I LOVE my Dymo 4XL laser printer. I bought it refurbished for $80 and I never have to buy ink cartridges, so it has paid for itself many times over. The 4XL prints Mercari shipping on 4x6" sticker labels, so you don't have to cut labels out or tape them onto the package – just stick 'em on and go. There is a trick to get the Mercari labels to print correctly on the 4XL labels. If you just print from the downloaded Mercari label, it prints very small and the bar code is not scannable by USPS or FedEx. To get the shipping label set up for the 4XL, right-click on the label 'preview' page (not the downloaded label). After you right-click, select 'Save As' and then save a copy of the preview form to your desktop. Next, 'Open In' your photo editor and rotate the item, so that fits correctly on the label (spin it to vertical orientation, instead of horizontal). Then, click 'Print' and make sure that the 4XL is selected as your active printer. Good to go. Once you do this once, it only takes a couple of seconds to make the adjustment.

Saving Money on Packaging and Shipping: There are several excellent articles on how to properly package and ship items sold on internet sites on our blog at www.ericmichaelbooks.com. Every internet seller quickly learns how important it is to ensure that customers receive their items exactly as they appear in the item listing or auction. Nothing will get you a negative feedback or rating faster than to ship a valuable item to a customer in subpar packaging, especially if it breaks. Damaged shipments can also significantly affect your profits, when you have process refunds to cover damaged items.

It is a fact of the internet selling business that you will have to buy packaging and shipping supplies. The trick is to minimize the overall costs of the overhead.   My first tip is to save packaging when you receive shipments in the mail. Most of us regularly buy stuff online, so you will have a steady flow of free shipping supplies. I keep sturdy boxes, packing peanuts, bubble wrap and padded envelopes to reuse for internet sales. You can also ask your friends, family and neighbors to save boxes for you, when you get to the point that you need a bunch of boxes for shipments. This can save you hundreds of dollars very easily. A medium sized supply of empty boxes can cost $50, including shipping fees if bought from shipping supply stores.

Tip #2 – Use free USPS boxes and envelopes. You can pick up free Priority Mail and Flat Rate Priority boxes and envelopes at any post office, or USPS will ship them to you for free from the USPS website! Why pay for boxes and envelopes when USPS will give them to you for free?

Tip #3 – Buy shipping supplies in bulk online. You can greatly reduce the cost of shipping and packaging supplies by buying large shipments of things that you will be using a lot for your business. I buy most of my shipping supplies in bulk lots on eBay. Here are some of the items that can be bought in bulk to save lots of green: Boxes, packing tape, strapping tape, printer cartridges and bubble wrap.

MERCARI PHOTOGRAPHY

Your item photographs are vital to sell-through percentage of your items and to earn top profit for your goods on Mercari, which is even more visually-oriented than other internet sales outlets. It is worth taking some extra time and effort to have great photos, especially the main item photo that is displayed to customers in search results and on browsing pages.

Many Mercari sellers are lazy. They take one photo or use a stock photo of their item and that is it! Their laziness can be to your benefit, especially after you get more experienced at posting items and taking great item photos.

Before we continue, I mentioned stock photos. Using stock photos copied from Google images or Amazon is not only bad for sales, it is also against Mercari's Terms of Service and can get your item deleted or worse – get your seller account suspended. Besides that, would you buy an item without seeing an actual photo of the item? Using stock photos is stupid.

OK, let's get back to uploading photos. The first thing to realize is that Mercari photos are square, while most cell phone cameras take oblong shaped photos. Most of the time, I just take standard photos with my cell phone and then crop the photo to get the view that I want from the Mercari listing page. You can also use a photo editor to produce a square photo or use an such as Instagram Layout or MOLDIV to size your photos.

When you are uploading the photos to Mercari, the first photo that you upload is the default main item photo. You can move photos around later and choose a different main photo by click-and-dragging them on the listing page, if you like. You can either take your photos while you are listing and upload as you go, or you can take the photos ahead of time and upload from your phone's file manager or photo app.

The best aspect of Mercari's photo uploader is the photo verification feature. After you upload your photo, you can see exactly what your photo will look like, so you can tell if it is in focus and displaying the portion of your item that you want in the item photo. You can easily discard the photo and replace it with a new one, if there are any issues with the initial photograph.

There is tons of information available on the internet regarding how to take great photos for internet listings. We also have some good blog posts on photography, so I am not going to rehash that information here. But, it extremely important to have a main photograph that is in focus, has proper lighting and is positioned so that customers can see what the item is (proper zoom). Remember, for most popular types of items, there will be dozens of other sellers trying to sell the same item at the same time on Mercari. Nothing will prevent a sale faster than having a main photo that is super dark or out of focus.

Photo Tips that will Sell More Items:

1. Differentiate your listing from other similar listing by using a different angle or zooming in on the aspect of your item that is the most attractive to your buyer. For instance, if you are selling Madden 18, you could focus your main item photo on the football star on the cover, instead of using a photo of the whole case like most other sellers do.
2. Upload extra photos of your item. Many sellers only use one photo. At the very least, take a photo of the back of the item. For many media items and board games, the back of the item has additional features that are attractive to buyers.
3. Know who your main target audience is and entice them with your photo.
4. Use an In-Action photo that shows how functional your item is or how much fun it is to play, etc. Think outside the box. Photos of people wearing clothes are much more attractive than photos of a garment lying on a table.
5. The background in the photo matters! Ensure that you don't have distracting things going on behind your item. And for goodness sakes, make sure that you don't have dirty dishes, pets or food in the background (I've seen them all in Mercari photos). You can use photo editing apps to remove all background noise and use a white or black background behind the item.
6. Light boxes are great tools for small items like jewelry. You can buy them on eBay or Amazon for a reasonable cost.
7. Make sure that your photos allow the customer to judge the condition of used items. If you discuss a defect in the description, you should also provide a photo of that part of the item, so the customer can make an informed buying decision.
8. Use bright colors and nice texture contrasts that will catch the eye when viewed on a browsing page. If your item has drab colors, you can use a brighter color in the background. I keep a variety of colored fabrics for using as backgrounds behind my items when photographing them.
9. Try not to use people's faces in item photos. You want potential customers to be able to imagine themselves owning and using your item, not somebody else.

Chapter Summary:

Photos are vital to the sales price and sell-through rate of Mercari items
- Upload multiple photos, not just one
- Make sure photos are in focus and have proper lighting
- Show the best aspect of your photo in the main item photo
- Make your item stand out in search results by using colorful backgrounds or contrasting textures
- Market to your target audience with your photos

CATEGORIES OF USED ITEMS TO SELL

I would like to talk to you about what to look for while you are shopping for inventory items at garage sales, yard sales, flea markets and thrift stores and provide you with some tips that will help you to find high value items at very low prices.

<u>Books</u>:

Books are easy to sell on Amazon and can be very profitable, which is why so many existing Amazon sellers specialize in selling them. Books are available at almost every yard sale and thrift store, and they are usually affordable. Plus, some older books are collectible and valuable. You will regularly find $20 books wherever you look for Amazon inventory.

The EMB Used Books page has many tips for how to find high priced books to add to your inventory, but here are some highlights:

- Use a Smart Phone with the Amazon Price Check application. This takes the guess-work out of deciding which used books to buy for profit. You scan the book with your Smart phone, and the app tells you what the book is selling for on Amazon.
- Used textbooks can be sold for excellent profits. If you have bought textbooks lately, you know that even used texts can cost $150. But, you have to be careful buying textbooks without the Amazon Price Check app. Many titles are updated yearly, so if you have a textbook that is two or three years old, it may be outdated and worthless.
- Many sellers look for hardcover books and textbooks to sell for profit, but I have well over 100 softcover books in my Amazon inventory worth over $50, and several over $100. Look for rare titles, softcover texts, vintage pulp fiction titles, and very thin books. Many of these vintage books with less than 40 pages are rare and collectible.

- If you look at a book and think "Who in the heck would want to read that?!" it is probably rare and valuable. Buy it. Some of the highest priced books in my inventory are not first edition classics, they are rare paperbacks: Flood Hazards in Virginia - $195, The Thrift Store Prospector - $195.60, Answers to the Space Flight Challenge - $145. All three of these books are thin vintage softcover books found for under $1.
- Condition is very important. Books with condition problems like broken hinges, missing pages, and modern books with missing dust jackets can make the books worthless for resale.
- Check all free boxes at yard sales for books and media items. Take EVERY book that you can find for free. The worst case scenario is that you have to donate the items to Goodwill later. I have found many $20 books in free boxes.

Music:

Used music such as CDs, vinyl records and even 8-tracks, cassettes, and other vintage formats can be sold on Amazon. Some collectible vinyl record and CD titles can be worth thousands of dollars, but it is very rare to find these at second-hand stores.

Selling used music is a competitive business. Everybody loves music. Still, you can make good money selling used CDs and records, if you know what to look for and how to sell them. Many used music internet sellers hang out on eBay for some reason, which gives Amazon sellers a big advantage.

Amazon allows you to list inventory for free. EBay also has tens of thousands of used music items at auction at any given time. Tons of quality items never get bids on eBay. The same item can be listed for free on Amazon, sell for a higher price, and sellers are given a $3.99 shipping credit.

Here is a selection of helpful tips for buying used music for profit:

- Don't be tempted to buy music that you like for $2+. Many popular titles on CD are 'penny CDs'. Remember, millions of these CDs were printed, and many CDs are being tossed in favor of MP3 files. There is an overabundance of many pop titles at second hand locations and on Amazon, which makes many excellent used CDs almost worthless to sell on Amazon.
- Use Amazon Price Check app.

- Look for rare CDs, and classical titles. Vintage blues and jazz CDs can also be valuable.
- Pick up any CDs that are sealed and you can sell on Amazon as 'New'.
- Grab any CDs that you see in free boxes. Even CDs without cases can be sold on Amazon.
- Check all CDs before you buy them. Ensure that the CD is in the case, as thieves often steal the disc and leave the case, especially at thrift stores. Also, check for large surface scratches, missing artwork, and broken case hinges.
- Keep a supply of replacement cases on hand. I often swap out cases with broken hinges, broken CD holders, or surface cracks.

Video Games and DVDs

Used video games can be excellent sellers on Amazon! It is common to find used video game systems for $10 or less at second-hand locations, and many vintage systems will sell for $30-70 when packaged with the cords, controllers and a couple of games.

It would be well worth your time to scan through the video game system category on Amazon, so that you have a good idea what each system is currently selling for.

Become familiar with what the power cords and AV cords for video game systems look like, so you can pick them up when you see them at garage sales or thrift stores. I have found a lot of cords for 25 cents at garage sales, packed in with big bags of cords at thrift stores, and even in free boxes. You never know when you will find a system that is missing a cord.

Just last week, I found an original PlayStation at a thrift store for $4. It had no cords or controllers with it, which is why it was priced so cheaply. I took it home, dug through my 'random cords box', and found a PlayStation 1 power cord, AV cord and two controllers.

I found all of these accessories in free boxes at garage sales over the years. I tested the PlayStation, and it worked great. I listed it on Amazon and it sold yesterday for $25. If I would have had some PS1 games to package with the system, I could have earned another $5 to $10.

Both DVDs and video games are constantly upgrading in technology. The newest video game system titles can bring $40 used and sell the same day that Amazon sellers list them. That is why it can really pay to have your Smart phone with you. These newer video games will not be $1 or $2. But, even if you have to pay $10 for a $30 title with high demand, you win.

DVDs are getting harder to make money on, unless you are selling on Amazon FBA. Many tech-savvy consumers are opting to buy movies by streaming them on their computers and most people now get movies sent to their homes via Netflix.

This is especially true of newer titles that are available in Blu-ray. Many used standard DVDs are penny DVDs, when the same title is now available on Blu-ray.

Look for older DVDs that were not re-released on Blu-ray. Popular TV series DVD sets also sell well. We hit a home run about three years ago when the local hospital gave their nurses free copies of vintage TV show DVD sets. Several of our friends gave us their copies, and we found quite a few more at thrift stores, still in the shrink-wrap. Several of the sets sold for almost $100, and the single episodes sold for $20-30. Bingo!

Some other DVDs to look for: Director's cuts, Collector's Sets of popular titles and classics, Remastered DVDs, rare titles that you have never heard of, cult classics, and vintage sports DVDs. I have also done very well with rare concert DVDs, especially if you can find early concerts of popular bands or punk rock / thrash concerts.

You can also occasionally make some money on rare VHS tapes, but they sell slowly and most of them are not worth much. If you can get them for free… take them, of course.

Used Toys and Board Games:

Selling used toys and games on Mercari and Amazon is a nice racket.

Pay attention to the toys aisles while you are at Meijer, K-Mart and Wal-Mart so that you know what toys are titled and which toys are expensive to buy at stores. Those are the toys that you will look for while at second-hand stores and garage sales.

Even loose action figures, Hot Wheels, Barbie dolls, and other small toys can be sold in used condition. Used toys can often take some time to sell, but you can also get these toys for very cheap. If you have young kids like we do, outgrown toys can become profit makers in your Amazon inventory, especially large outdoor toys and electronic toys.

We have sold many used toys that our boys have outgrown. Kids also learn about the value of keeping toys in good condition. We let our boys sell their own toys to upgrade to new ones, but the toys that are in poor condition or missing pieces… sorry, boys.

Used board games can also be sold effectively sold on Mercari. Some are worth $50+. In the last couple of years, I have sold four sealed board games found at thrift stores for over $50, including an original Trivial Pursuit for $80 that was sold in two days. The vintage 3M bookshelf games also sell for good profits – usually over $20.

Some other games to look for: Electronic board games, vintage versions of classic games and handheld electronic games.

Household and Decorative Items:

I have sold a wide array of used household items found at garage sales and thrift stores. Newer decorative items that are sold at popular department stores often sell fairly quickly on Amazon. Some categories of items that I have sold online and made good money: electronics, prints, utensils, clocks, and holiday decorations (Halloween décor sells for higher prices than Christmas, for some reason).

Understand that many used household items sell very slowly, and you will have to store them for a while. Many of these items are larger and bulkier than media items, so you will need more room than you would for books or CDs.

Chapter Summary:

Types of used items that can be found for cheap and sold on Mercari for high profit margins:
- Books
- Music
- Video Games
- Toys and Games
- Household Items
- New sealed items with barcodes

INCREASE PROFITS AND SELL ITEMS FASTER BY MAKING BETTER ITEM DESCRIPTIONS ON MERCARI

It never ceases to amaze me how lazy some people are. I always look at other sellers' item descriptions while I am listing my own items. There are many sellers who do not even bother to type in a description of their item, or its condition!

A typical Mercari item will have dozens of similar listings from other sellers. Besides the price, there are only two things that customers can look at to determine which seller they will buy the item from. The first is the seller's rating, which is displayed beside the seller's name. We will talk about seller ratings and your reputation on Mercari later.

The second thing that customers look at is the item description.

Keep in mind that there are typically multiple listings that will be priced within $1 of each other, so the item description is often what sells the item to the costumer. Still, there many listings that do not have a description at all, or just a condition listing and price.

For us small to medium sized sellers, that is a huge advantage. By spending less than 30 seconds, you can set your listing apart from the other listings and make it much more likely to sell.

1. Describe the condition of the item. Do not rely on the Mercari condition guidelines. Most customers do have any idea what the guidelines are. Remember, your reputation is at stake, so make sure that your customers know what they are buying.
2. Give the customer even more confidence by giving them a short sales pitch. This should be saved as a text document, so that you can cut-and-paste it into each Amazon listing: 'Reliable and experienced book seller with thousands of satisfied customers. Items are securely packaged using dedicated mailers in bubble wrap.'

This whole listing would take you no more than 20-30 seconds to type and/or cut-and-paste. Yet, this listing will make your item much more likely to sell to the first couple of customers looking to buy your item in used condition.

Chapter Summary:

It is important to write good item descriptions
- Earn more sales by building customer confidence
- Prevent non-positive customer feedback

What does a good item description contain?
1. Verify item – Identification numbers, titles
2. Thorough condition description(s)
3. Build confidence in your business – safe shipping, experience
4. Keep important information first

MERCARI PRICING AND INVENTORY MANAGEMENT PRACTICES THAT YIELD MORE MERCARI SALES

Let's face it. Most people who buy used items do so in order to save some money over buying new items. What does that mean for the used item seller on Mercari?

In my opinion, you must price items to move. That means that many items should be priced at the lower end of the price range for the applicable condition subcategory for each item that is listed. About 75% of my inventory items are the lowest priced item in their condition subcategory.

On the surface, this may seem to be counterproductive to profits. Really, this strategy works well for several reasons. Number one, impulse buyers are going to pick the lowest priced used item that they are looking to buy, even if your item has a couple of minor condition issues. Number two, customers who choose the lowest priced items are not as picky as the customers who choose to upgrade to higher priced offerings. You will have fewer customer returns and negative feedbacks from customers who buy the lowest priced item that is offered.

This does not mean that if you have a high-priced collectible that is in excellent condition that you should lose profits by listing your item at a price that is cheaper than inferior products. This 'lowest price principle' only applies to identical items that are comparable in condition.

One trick that I have used for rare items with only a couple of listings is to set the price far above the lowest price. For instance, if I have a rare CD that only has one other listing at $5; I will often list my copy at $25. I have sold many items at the higher price using this method, as long as the description identifies the item well and specifies that it is collectible and rare. Sometimes, the $25 item will even sell before the $5 item, because the customer thinks that there is something wrong with the lower priced item. Even if the lower priced item sells first, you will still have the next lowest priced item at $25, so the next customer will have no choice – your $25 item, or nothing. This method works great.

You will have to manage your inventory periodically to keep your prices competitive with other sellers' listings.   After you have been adding items for a while, you will find that items that you listed as the lowest prices item in its condition subcategory are $1 or $2 above the lowest price. It is very common for other sellers to do exactly what you do… set the lowest price by condition.

Chapter Summary:

How to price your used items: Lowest price in condition subcategory sells more items and turns inventory over to make room for new items.

Approaches for inventory pricing management

1. Maintain the lowest price in the condition subcategory – Price matching
2. Set your best prices when you list items, and leave them
3. Hybrid – Limited price matching

CUSTOMER RELATIONS PRACTICES AND MAINTAINING A HIGH CUSTOMER FEEDBACK PERCENTAGE

There is no difference between the way you should treat a customer at a physical store and the way you should treat Mercari buyers. Keeping your customers happy is vital to your business. As we discussed in prior chapters, your positive feedback percentage is one of the first things that your potential customers will look at when deciding whether to buy goods from you.

Let's take a step back and I will explain Mercari's feedback process and what feedback means for your business.

Most people are familiar with the idea of feedback for internet purchases. EBay has been using customer feedback for years and it is integrated into their buying process. Mercari's feedback process is a little different than both eBay's and Amazon's.

Feedback is not specifically requested by Amazon. Buyers have to access their customer order page to find the link to leave feedback. Many Amazon buyers do not even know that there is a feedback system for Amazon purchases, which leads to a low percentage of buyers leaving ratings and reviews.

With the Mercari feedback model, customers are prompted to leave feedback within 24 hours of receiving the item, as part of the transaction process. After customers receive their package in the mail, Mercari notifies them that their item has been delivered. They are also sent an email that asks them to complete the process by rating their seller. After 24 hours, Mercari issues a 5-star feedback on the customer's behalf.

This results in a high percentage of transactions resulting in ratings for sellers, which is great! Even better, the rating form lends itself to five-star ratings. Buyers simply click on a row of stars to pick their rating. Rating comments are optional, so many buyers do not bother with them. Usually, unless there is a major problem with the item, buyers click the 5-star rating just to close out the transaction. This results in a lot of individual 5-star ratings for sellers, keeps the average rating high and provides insurance against one bad rating from ruining your business.

As on any other internet selling site, Mercari sellers should protect their positive feedback percentage at all costs. Do NOT take negative and neutral feedbacks lightly. If you do receive negative feedback, make every effort to contact your buyer and come to an agreement whereby they will remove their negative feedback.

Mercari provides a link with every transaction, so that you can contact your buyer. There is also a link provided from your profile page. I recommend the following approach when contacting customers… kiss butt.

Whoever said that "the customer is always right" is full of crap. 95% of the time, they are wrong. Most of the time, it is the customer who made the mistake by buying items without reading the condition description or looking at the photos.

Still, to protect your feedback rating, you must try to make buyers happy. You should try to explain the situation that led to the misunderstanding of the condition of the item and try to work it out with the buyer. The best way to get poor ratings removed is to have the customer request removal of the rating via Mercari Customer Care. Give the buyer clear directions for how to request a rating removal. They simply click on the link from the purchased item that says, 'Report an Issue with this Transaction' and request rating / feedback removal.

If communicating with your buyer does not work, Mercari customer care seems to be significantly more receptive to sellers' ratings and feedback removal requests than eBay or Amazon are. Many sellers have reported that Mercari has removed unwarranted poor ratings, if the reason that the buyer left a poor rating was their own fault (did not read descriptions, etc.). To request a seller removal of a rating, use the 'report a problem' link from the sold item and tell customer care why the rating was unfair. Surprisingly, so far Mercari has been receptive to removing poor ratings at sellers' requests.

As I mentioned before, even the best sellers of used items get negative feedbacks that cannot be removed. This is due in part to the nature of selling used items and the requirement of assigning subjective values, and partly because there are just a number of stupid people out there. Some people just are not going to be happy, no matter what you do. So be prepared to deal with the non-positive feedback(s), because you will receive them eventually.

Here are some steps that you can take to minimize negative feedbacks:

1. Accurately assign condition ratings. Describe condition issues completely in the text description when listing your items.
2. Answer your seller messages, ASAP. When you get messages, respond immediately. Nothing annoys people more than getting ignored.
3. Deal with non-positive feedbacks immediately, using the procedures described.
4. Don't list items with major flaws. I don't buy anything that I think should be rated as 'Poor', which is the lowest condition rating. Don't list anything that you would not like to receive in the mail yourself.
5. Put yourself in your potential customers' shoes. What would you want to know about the item before buying it? What aspects of the condition of the item would you want described to you? Make sure that you address these concerns in your item description.
6. Do not list your item in the wrong category.
7. Package your items securely, so they do not get damaged during shipping.
8. Consider enclosing a message with each item shipped, or send buyers a personal email with your logo on it. Explain how important customer satisfaction is to your business, and ask them to contact you if there are any condition issues prior to leaving feedback. I have always been undecided on whether to send additional messages regarding feedback. On one hand, you are showing your concern for customer satisfaction. On the other hand, you may be creating more problems for yourself by suggesting that there may possibly be issues with your product(s).

Chapter Summary:

It is vital to your Mercari business to keep customers happy!

1. Builds your business' reputation – High feedback rating = more sales
2. Earn return customers and word-of-mouth advertising
3. Reduces item returns and refunds

How to deal with unhappy customers

1. Return e-mails and messages ASAP
2. Kiss butt and show concern for their issue(s)

How to handle non-positive feedback (This is super important!)

1. Immediate e-mail message
2. Apologize, and tell the customer you value their opinion
3. Explain the value of your feedback rating, and how non-positive feedbacks significantly affect your business. Provide the 'Remove Feedback' instructions
4. If #3 does not work, send a second e-mail that offers a full refund.

HOW TO INCREASE SALES PRICE AND THE NUMBER OF SOLD ITEMS – MERCARI SELLING TIPS

OK, so now for the fun stuff. You've been selling for a little while and you want to make the next step. You want to make a significant income from your Mercari business. You want to streamline your activities and eliminate unsold items.

Here are some valuable Mercari selling tips:

1. Price your items higher than what you think they are worth. Mercari is a very hands-on sales platform. It's not like Amazon, where the price is firm, or eBay where the price is determined by bids. On Mercari, customers often send sellers offers below the sticker price. It is very common for sellers to receive multiple offers at the same time and items are often closed out below the sticker price by accepting offers. Mercari also has a 'Promote' feature, that allows sellers to automatically reduce the price 5% and be elevated in search results. Sellers can Promote up to 10 items at a time (items must be priced over $10 and can only be Promoted once every 3 days). So, sellers often start their items at a fairly high price, because they know the price is going to be reduced by promotions and offers.
2. Develop your seller profile. Upload a sharp looking logo for your company or clear personal photo and describe your business in the bio. Make it look like you know what you are doing. Earn all your seller badges, which as displayed in your items and give your customers confidence. You can earn a badge for being a confirmed seller, being a quick shipper (under 24-hour average to ship out items), being a fast responder (respond to questions within 12 hours on average) and being a reliable seller (minimal refunds and/or poor reviews).
3. Relist items if they do not sell within a week or so. Mercari Prohibited Conduct rules do prohibit sellers from "excessively re-posting the same item" or "creating

multiple listings for the same item", so you must vary your title, photos and/or description when you repost. Mercari's search engines reduce exposure for items that have been posted for a while and reward newly posted items with higher placement in search results. So, you can often sell items much faster if you make new listings for your unsold items (within reason – don't get yourself into trouble by re-posting the same listing once a day).

4. For lightning-quick sales, post your items during the best times for Mercari buying activity. Many sellers have had good luck posting items on the weekends or in the evening and sometimes late night after 11PM you can take advantage of reduced competition.

5. Upload quality main item photos and use multiple photos (at least three) to give your customers confidence in buying your item

6. Give your customers everything that they need to know in the item description. Describe the item in detail and describe the condition of the item to the best of your ability. Use spell-check to keep your description looking professional.

7. Make good use of your ten Promoted items. Rotate the promoted items so you are always featuring several of your high-end items for more exposure.

8. Ship items out as fast as you can, especially for your first several months of selling. Try to get packages out the next shipping day after your item is sold. You want to earn your Fast Shipping badge as quickly as possible and getting your items to customers faster will lead to higher ratings.

9. Offer some of your items with Free Shipping. Some customers only search for items with free shipping – it is a check box that can be selected when narrowing search parameters.

10. Sometimes, a small price drop or featuring an item that has multiple likes can yield a quick sale. When buyers Like an item, it is added to a populated list of their Liked items. When the price is reduced, some buyers will get a notification of the price drop on their phones. You can also send a personal message to the buyers that have Liked your item to notify them of the price drop but be cautious

with how often you send messages. You do not want to harass buyers and some people consider these types of messages as spam.

11. Focus on the types of items that sell the best on Mercari. Name brand used clothing with very light wear, the latest generation of video games and hot home décor brands sell very fast on Mercari. Don't risk your seller reputation on items that are not in good condition or missing parts. You also do not want to waste a lot of time listing a bunch of items that will not sell quickly or without multiple promotions.
12. If you have items that you feel should be selling but are not, change things up. Switch your main item photo and/or revise your title to add new keywords.

WHAT NOT TO DO ON MERCARI: TERMS OF SERVICE AND VIOLATIONS

Mercari prides itself on being a friendly platform for buying and selling, so it is a bit picky on regulating certain types of activities. Some of these regulations are not common sense, either.

Here are some of the important links to the Mercari selling regulations and terms of service:

https://www.mercari.com/help_center/getting_started/prohibited_conduct/

https://www.mercari.com/help_center/getting_started/prohibited_items/

https://www.mercari.com/help_center/getting_started/mercari_marketplace_guidelines/

Make sure that you read these guidelines carefully, because there are many prior Mercari sellers who have been permanently banned from selling for listing prohibited items. Listing items like sex toys, large knives or parts of weapons will quickly get you suspended.

Some items that are prohibited on Mercari can be sold legally on other high-profile internet selling platforms, so you must pay attention when you are thinking about listing certain types of items.

Mercari also seems to be particularly sensitive to certain types of descriptive words in item titles. I got one of my listings removed for including the word 'sexy' in the title of a woman's top. Pretty tame, eh?

Here are several other rules that you may be surprised to learn about:

- You must be 18 years old to sell on Mercari
- You cannot use "excessive amount of search keywords". I have no idea exactly what this means or what excessive is, but you should not use only keywords in your title. Make your title look natural (don't "keyword stuff").
- You cannot "excessively repost previously listed items". As we discussed before, it is to sellers' benefit to relist items that are not being sold quickly. You must change the title and/or the photos when you relist to avoid getting in trouble for violating this rule.

- You cannot have multiple Mercari accounts
- You cannot use stock photos or photos that were not taken by you in your items
- You cannot sell any type of alcohol, tobacco items or accessories, FDA regulated items like vitamins and muscle powders, anything illegal, anything "vulgar or offensive", any sex related items, any firearms, ammunition or firearm accessories, any hand-made items that use trademarked logos, any digital items (must a physical item, not an item such as an e-book or PDF file).
- You cannot sell anything that is not in your physical possession. Drop-shipping is a violation and will lead to suspension.
- You cannot sell any type of "knock-off" items, which are lower cost items made to look like high-end items. You cannot sell any counterfeit or replica items on Mercari.

The first rule on the list of prohibited behaviors is not the rule about posting prohibited items. DO NOT try to sell something that may be determined to be a prohibited item by a conservative person. All it takes is for one buyer to report your item to Mercari Customer Care and you have a good chance of being suspended. When in doubt, DO NOT LIST IT.

DIVERSIFYING YOUR MERCARI BUSINESS: SELLING PRODUCTS ON AMAZON, CRAIGSLIST, EBAY AND ETSY

A good internet seller does not limit themselves to selling on only one venue. There are many different ways to sell used items and sellers can take advantage of the benefits each location provides.

Although I believe that Mercari and Amazon are by far the best overall locations to sell the types of goods that I sell, there are times when it is easier or more productive to sell my items on other sites.

For instance, there are going to be times when you want to sell items with a quick turnaround. Perhaps you have a family vacation coming up, or you want to make a large purchase.

EBay almost guarantees a sale within a week, if you set the starting price low enough to encourage bidding. You can even make your auction shorter to decrease the time it takes to get payment for your items – you can make 3-Day or even 1-Day listings.

EBay also has the following benefits, when compared to selling on Mercari and Amazon:

1. Often shorter time to get your money – 1 day to 1 week.
2. There is always the potential to have your auction make more money than you thought the item was worth. If you get the right situation and have multiple bidders who really want your item, you can make a lot of extra money.
3. Visually appealing items benefit from additional photos on eBay
4. Some categories of items cannot be sold on Mercari or Amazon or sell very slowly. For instance, vintage used clothing can make a lot of money on eBay, but cannot be sold on Amazon.

I use eBay infrequently, but there are advantages to listing items in an auction setting there from time to time.

Etsy.com is another internet location that specializes is vintage items, arts and crafts and craft supplies. Etsy is an excellent location to sell retro and mid-century items, which you can often find at garage sales for cheap. These items can sell for hundreds of dollars on Etsy. Etsy is set up much like eBay Fixed Price listings. You make a listing like on eBay, and provide photos. Your listing is active for 3 months for twenty cents.

I also use Craigslist for selling large items that would cost too much to ship on Mercari or eBay. Craigslist listings are free, and there is also the advantage to avoiding the hassle of packaging and shipping large or very fragile items.

Chapter Summary:

How and when to diversify your used item sales using other websites
1. eBay – see below
2. Etsy for vintage, retro, and arts & crafts
3. Craigslist for large, heavy, or very fragile items to avoid shipping

When eBay may be a better choice to sell used items:
1. Certain used items cannot be sold effectively on Amazon e.g. Used clothes
2. Visually appealing collectibles benefit from more photos and more detailed descriptions
3. When you think that an eBay auction setting may yield many bids and possibly a higher price than a set price Mercari or Amazon listing
4. When Amazon's shipping allowance does not cover actual shipping costs – set your own shipping fees on your eBay auction.
5. When you want money fast. eBay auctions end in 1,3,5, or 7 days (10 days at an increased cost).

ADDITIONAL LINKS FOR FURTHER RESEARCH

Eric Michael Author Central Page

'Almost Free Money' books for Internet Resellers:

1) Almost Free Money, Volume 1 FREE! (#1 Kindle bestseller, Top 10 for 3 years running). Learn how to find over 500 different types of items for free where you live and sell for profit online and at scrap metal locations for big bucks.

2) Thrift Wars (#1 Kindle Bestseller): Learn how professional sellers locate the best items to resell from thrift stores for very high profit margins. Learn how to sell on Amazon, Etsy and eBay for maximum profit margins.

3) Etsy Empire (#1 Kindle and Softcover bestseller, top 10 for 8 months straight): How to build a powerful Etsy shop and sell handmade and collectible items on Etsy.com. Master Etsy SEO, social media for Etsy and Etsy marketing with a proven step-by-step formula.

4) Etsy Empire Strikes Back (#1 Kindle Bestseller): Advanced techniques for marketing with social media, like Facebook, Instagram and Pinterest, plus the latest Etsy shop rules and updates

5) Almost Free Gold: (#1 Kindle bestseller, top 10 for 12 months straight): Learn how to find valuable gold and silver jewelry for cheap at garage sales and thrift stores. You can also learn how to harvest free gold and silver from junk sources in this fun and unique approach to earning income!

6) The Almost Free Money Triple Play Value Pack: Contains the three bestselling AFM books: Almost Free Money, Passive Income for Life and Garage Sale Superstar. A great bargain!

7) Fast Cash: Selling Used Items for Profit: (#1 Kindle and Softcover bestseller) Learn how to find the best items at second-hand locations and build your own business on Amazon, eBay and Etsy.

8) Garage Sale Superstar: (#1 Kindle bestseller and Top 10 for 12 months): Learn how to make the most profit possible at your next garage sale. Tips on organizing, advertising and pricing at garage sales, yard sales and estate sales.

THANK YOU, READERS!

Thank you for taking the time to read this book. I hope that you enjoyed it as much as I enjoyed writing it.

Please put your mind to immediately applying what you learned in this book. Don't wait until next week to start! You can find items to sell in any location, and at any time of the year.

YOU have to make up your mind to start selling used items on Amazon, and it will be all increasing profits from there. I wish you success in building your passive income through Amazon.

Click on the link below to join the Almost Free Money Nation. This free newsletter provides exclusive free white papers and advance reading chapters from unreleased AFM books, free tips and tricks to help you find great items at second-locations and learn how to sell them, and links to new Garage Sale Academy webpages.

http://forms.aweber.com/form/75/228725575.htm

If you have any questions, please contact me at the Almost Free Money Facebook page, on Twitter, or email me at almostfreemoney@yahoo.com. I would enjoy hearing from you!

If you feel that this book has helped you to find new and enjoyable ways to make a new passive income for you and your family, I humbly ask you for only two things. #1, tell your family and friends about this book, and #2, please take several seconds to leave positive feedback for this book on its Amazon Detail Page. After all, you should be able to easily make 1000 times the $3 that you spent on this book in your first year of selling.

Positive feedback directly affects other readers' reviews and leads to additional orders, and the proceeds from this book will go directly into my sons' college funds. Thanks again, and happy hunting!

Thrift Wars: *A Battle-Tested Internet Business Plan: Find Hidden Thrift Stores Treasure and Sell on Amazon, eBay and Etsy for Huge Profits with Online Arbitrage* is now updated on Amazon Kindle.

Thrift Wars is the first true Thrift Store flipping manual and includes hands-on experience finding a huge variety of thrift store items and selling them for maximum profit on eBay, Amazon, Amazon FBA, Etsy and Classified sites.

Topics: The best thrifts to shop, how to buy low and sell high, maximizing per-item profit, improving online listings and photos on eBay and Amazon, diversification across multiple internet sales venues, identification of high-end collectibles and sales items, locating gold and silver at thrift shops and much more. The book is illustrated with rescued thrift store treasures and their online sales prices.

Readers' Praise for *Almost Free Money*

5.0 out of 5 stars

The author is a money-making machine

By **Bill Nelson**

This review is from: **Almost Free Money: How to Make Extra Money on Free Items That You Can Find Anywhere, Including Garage Sales, Thrift Shops, Scrap Metal and Finding Gold (Kindle Edition)**

"This guy is like a money-making machine. Almost Free Money: How to Make Significant Money on Free Items That You Can Find Anywhere, Including Garage Sales, Scrap Metal, and Discarded Items by Eric Michael is yet another goldmine of information on how to make money!

Seriously, whether you want to earn some extra cash in your spare time or want to make a career out of buying and selling, this book (and several others by the same author) will get you going, and keep you there. The appendix is worth the price of the book but every page contains valuable tips and pointers. Highly recommended 5-stars."

5.0 out of 5 stars

This is a great book! It contains lots of ideas on how to make money from surprising places

By **Steven Johnson "Publisher of debt and credit"**

This review is from: **Almost Free Money: How to Make Extra Money on Free Items That You Can Find Anywhere, Including Garage Sales, Thrift Shops, Scrap Metal and Finding Gold (Kindle Edition)**

"This is a great book! It contains lots of ideas on how to make money from surprising places, and the resource directory at the back of the book is worth 10x the price of this book all by itself. Highly recommended. I like the way the author told how he got started in this type of business, and his advice on what to sell as scrap, what to sell as collectible, and what to sell as utilitarian, everyday use, was very interesting. I'm sure that as I visit thrift shops and garage sales in the future, this book will help me identify many new items that will make me money!"

Readers' Praise for Almost Free Gold!

5.0 out of 5 stars **Informative and very helpful!**

Sammy K. (Galveston, TX)

This review is from: Almost Free Gold!: How to Earn a Quick $1000 Finding Gold, Silver and Platinum Where You Live (Almost Free Money) (Kindle Edition)

> "I have been picking at yard sales and thrift stores for years and have used several of the other books in this series with success, including Almost Free Money. I learned a lot that I didn't know from Almost Free Gold. For me, the most valuable portions of the book were the methods for finding hidden gold and sterling at yard sales. I've got lots of new places to look and now I know how to find the stuff that other pickers have missed! I am also planning on taking the author's advice and contacting some of the businesses mentioned for setting up consistent sources of precious metals. Plus, you have to check out the chapter on the metal that is more valuable than gold! Fascinating stuff and the basis for a new hobby / business / addiction combination!"

Copyright, Legal Notice and Disclaimer:

This publication is protected under the US Copyright Act of 1976 and all other applicable international, federal, state and local laws, and all rights are reserved, including resale rights: you are not allowed to give or sell this Guide to anyone else.

Please note that much of this publication is based on personal experience and anecdotal evidence. Although the author and publisher have made every reasonable attempt to achieve complete accuracy of the content in this document, they assume no responsibility for errors or omissions. Also, you should use this information as you see fit, and at your own risk. Your particular situation may not be exactly suited to the examples illustrated here; in fact, it's likely that they won't be the same, and you should adjust your use of the information and recommendations accordingly.

Any trademarks, service marks, product names or named features are assumed to be the property of their respective owners, and are used only for reference. There is no implied endorsement if we use one of these terms.

Finally, use your head. Nothing in this Guide is intended to replace common sense, legal, medical or other professional advice, and is meant to inform and entertain the reader.

Copyright © 2018 Eric Michael. All rights reserved worldwide

© **Almost Free Money, Volume 10**

www.ingramcontent.com/pod-product-compliance
Lightning Source LLC
Chambersburg PA
CBHW030512220526
45464CB00006B/2762